Amy Peoples

Wearing Your Sanctuary:

Jewellery Design for Mental Wellbeing

An imprint of Boom Publications Ltd

272 Bath Street
Glasgow SCOTLAND
G2 4JR

Boom Graduates and the logo are trademarks of Boom Publications Ltd.

Boom Publications Ltd is a more-than-profit company, dedicating over half
our profits to university scholarships for underprivileged students worldwide.
In order to offset our carbon footprint, we also pledge to plant a tree for each
graduation book commissioned.

Wearing Your Sanctuary: Jewellery Design for Mental Wellbeing
was first published in Great Britain in 2022.

Boom Publications Ltd do not have any control over, or responsibility for any
third-party websites referred to or in this book. All internet addresses given in
this book were correct at the time of going to press. The author and publisher
regret any inconvenience if addresses have changed or sites have ceased to
exist, but can accept no responsibility for any such changes.

Typeset by Helen at Boom Graduates.
Printed and bound in the UK.

To find out more about our authors and books visit www.boomgraduates.com
and sign up for our newsletters.

Amy Peoples

We plant a tree for every
Boom Graduate book commissioned, and
thereafter plant a tree for every 10 books sold.

Watch our forest grow at
https://moretrees.eco/forest/BoomPublicationsLtd/

Amy Peoples

Wearing Your Sanctuary:

Jewellery Design
for Mental Wellbeing

Dedication

To my family and friends

And my beautiful godmother up in the clouds

Contents

List of Figures

---

[1] Available at: https://janeloren.com/products/loren-anti-anxiety-spinner-ring?variant=39626337353817 [Last Accessed: 21st January 2022]

Figure 9 - Spinner ring - Orli Jewellery (2022) Sterling Silver Spinner Ring With Gold Bands[2]

Figure 10 - screenshot from Harriet Kelsall Bespoke Jewellery website; Harriet Kelsall Bespoke Jewellery (2022) home page [Screenshot].[3]

Figure 11 - Logo for People in the Clouds

Figure 12 - Proposed Business Model Canvas (BMC) for People in the Clouds

Figure 13 - Drawing in Diary Study by case study participant

Figure 14 - User Journey Map of case study

Figure 15 - pie chart of Affinity Testing survey no.1

---

[2] Available at; https://www.orlijewellery.com/products/sterling-silver-spinner-ring-with-yellow-gold-bands?variant=39515711471719&utm_campaign=gs-2018-09-21&utm_source=google&utm_medium=smart_campaign&gclid=CjwKCAiA0KmPBhBqEiwAJqKK47CU_BsZ_fnMXFb5m-H1U8oM37l8azkYC2fbgPDiVTTknh_7DlHmbxoC3KcQAvD_BwE [Last accessed: 21st January 2022]

[3] Available at: https://www.hkjewellery.co.uk/ (Accessed: 22nd January 2022).

Figure 16 - pie chart of Affinity Testing survey no.2

Author biography

Originally from the southside of Glasgow Amy Peoples moved to Dundee in 2019 to study a Bachelor of Design (with Honours) in Jewellery and Metal Design. Through playing with alternative materials she discovered new methods of capturing memories of places into her jewellery.

Since graduating in June 2022 she has gone on to; present her work at New Designers 2022 (Week One) where she was shortlisted for New Designer of the Year; be named 'One to Watch' by Bright Young Gems; received the William Sangster Phillips Scholarship Award for her Masters of Fine Arts (Art, Science and Visual Thinking) at Duncan of Jordanstone College of Art and Design; exhibit at Elements Festival 2022; and invited to talk at the V&A's Upstart Creative Careers Festival.

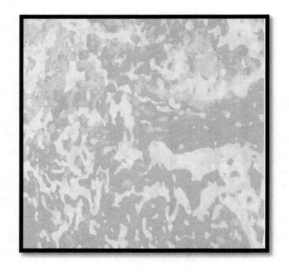

Figure 1 – Photo of sea at Brighouse Bay from Case Study

Executive Summary

This book has been written to explore a gap in the market for a company using natural materials from places of emotional connection to the wearer, with the aim of the wearer using the piece to enhance mindfulness practices in day-to-day life. This was sparked by an interest in both self-care and designing truly bespoke jewellery. There are several reasons why this is important; namely that there has been a sharp rise in conversation around mental health issues and looking into less medication-focused interventions of improving it. In addition, the fact that there are less restrictions regarding jewellery when uniforms are required.

Using a case study as a practice run for how the procedure would work in a business, a participant took part in the interview and design process which was specifically tailored around them.

Information was gathered on both historical and contemporary implications of using natural materials within jewellery design. This has been shown to potentially increase the value of a piece in a contemporary market. Jewellery has been shown to have emotional connections to their wearers both in the context that they were received or the actual design themselves. Comparatively fast fashion jewellery has been said to ignore this theme. But recent interest in climate change and sustainability issues have led many to revert to traditional views of jewellery being a more expensive, meaningful gift.

Mindfulness is being orated as an alternative to modern medicines being used to improve mental health. It does not require specific training or the use of professional time and so is more accessible than professional services due to long wait times. Similarly, acupressure and reflexology are more traditional medicines that do not require any specific tools also showing to have zero adverse effects. Harnessing the benefits of both could increase mental health in daily life.

The first interview was conducted with someone who has practised mindfulness for most of their lives. Producing insightful information about the potential benefits of mindfulness when practiced correctly, and their expertise on who it should be practiced by different people. How a blanket approach, such as used by apps like headspace, is not as effective as personalised mindfulness, tailored to the user's own experiences and surroundings.

Whereas the second interview was with somebody who works – while continuing to study - psychology in a professional manner. Whilst they personally believe that there are benefits to mindfulness and have direct experience with reflexology regarding physical health; they believe that mindfulness is part of what's known as pop psychology. Being very much misconstrued as something that is taught undergraduate level psychology.

A survey sent out over social media showed the lack of knowledge and understanding of the use of pressure points and what their benefits are. Said survey also garnered information on the jewellery wearing habits in a vast group of people.

A wide range of companies are now turning to more bespoke outlooks as part of their business models. Including areas such as fashion design, production design and online services/software. This is only growing in popularity.

An example of a popular jewellery item, a spinner ring, was compared when looking at the marketing of similar products from two different jewellery brands. Highlighting the importance of marketing and advertising.

A discussion took place with a pre-existing bespoke jewellery company to prove the validity of this sector. And how to become successful in current markets. Which backed up information sound when researching more general bespoke companies.

An idea for a company that fills this gap in the market is *People in The Clouds*. To show the start of a business plan a business model canvas was completed- as this is only at project proposal stage certain areas were missed out as it is not at the business proposal stage yet.

Circling back to the case study; a diary study that had been filled out by the participant throughout the course was analysed to gain insight into the effectiveness of the piece on her mindfulness habits. This perfectly encapsulated their thoughts and feelings inspired by the pendant designed around their special place.

Finally, a short survey acting as an affinity test was shared to validate whether there was a general interest in the idea. This also included a rough idea of what people are willing to spend for such an item.

Preface

One thing that this book doesn't cover is why I believe People in the Clouds' work is so important. From a young age the idea of neuro-divergence has been circling my mind, growing up with an older sibling with autism spectrum disorder (then classed as Asperger's Syndrome) allowed me to realise the variety of ways people can 'think differently'. Throughout my time at secondary school I volunteered in the school's Autism Unit (now Language and Communication Resource) which, on a personal note, re-enhanced that no two people have exactly the same sensory triggers. Rather, we are all told the same old wives' treatments fits everyone – something that would never be considered for physical variations in people. This does not just stand for ASD. As someone who has wrestled with severe anxiety, I have encountered the same one-size-fits-all blanket approaches.

When I spiral, I go down a sink hole. There is no side exit – I need a branch to pull me out. A physical artefact to clasp. To pull me up to solid ground. Why not use a branch that means something to me? Bring me back up to a place I love?

Visualising a specific place can be tough depending on how your mind learns, if you can't reach something physically you use a step. So why not have a step for your mind?

People in the Clouds' ethos has been created to solve these questions. Creating work for all ages – cutting out the stigma attached to classic 'fidget jewellery' designed for young children and allowing for a more subtle, intimate artefact to take its place.

Research Aim and Objectives

Aim:

To explore how by incorporating natural, found materials -from specific locations of emotional value into bespoke jewellery- creates an effective tool to evoke mindfulness practices to improve mental health in daily life; and how this could also lead to a viable business venture.

Objectives:

- to understand the impact of mindfulness, acupressure and reflexology on mental health

- to research the use of natural materials in contemporary jewellery design

- to research pre-existing bespoke businesses

- to carry out a case study to consider the benefits of the aim

Methodology

Case Study

To determine the validity of the hypothesis a case study has been conducted. The structure of the case study was as follows; initial interview of participant to discuss their chosen place; a visit to the place to gather natural materials; design and make a piece of jewellery based on the participant's style incorporating said natural materials; giving the item of jewellery to the participant to wear; user will keep a diary study of their mindful interacts with the piece to determine the effect it has on their daily mindfulness practices. During the initial semi-structured interview, information concerning the participants chosen place showed why there was a deep emotional connection to said place. As well as determining what items of jewellery they commonly wear, and what styles they prefer. This information allowed a bespoke piece of jewellery containing natural materials from the specific place of meaning to the participant to be designed to meet all their ergonomic and aesthetic wants and needs. An issue raised with this method was travelling to the specific place (Brighouse Bay), as it was a fair distance to travel. Meaning it took longer for the natural found materials could be collected.

Persona

A persona was created to show general information about the case study participant.

Interview (a)

To understand the theory of mindfulness on a deeper level an interview with someone who has practiced most of their lives was conducted. This was a semi-structured interview which took place in a cosy, café setting as both interviewer and interviewee were comfortable to talk freely creating less pressure. The aim of the interview was to determine what effect mindfulness has had on their life and why they believe it to be an important practice that should be used by others. Thus understanding more about the mindfulness practices that can be evoked by jewellery using natural materials from specific places of meaning.

Interview (b)

To understand the impact of mindfulness on mental health from a more clinical point of view an interview took place with a member of the University of Dundee's Psychology Department. This was to determine any potential arguments against mindfulness which could have been solved during the design process of jewellery using natural materials from specific places of meaning. The researcher in question was also asked about any knowledge and/or experience with acupressure and reflexology. It turns out that they did have personal experience with both and provided detailed insight into how these traditional medicine practices can be beneficial in both diagnoses and treatment of pain.

Survey

In order to discover what knowledge people have of pressure points, their fidgeting habits and what jewellery they tend to wear a survey was created, posted over social media and shared to various online groups. An issue with this type of research is that the group of participants come from a vast number of different backgrounds, providing widespread results.

Interview (c)

To gain a professional insight into the viability of a bespoke centred jewellery company – an online interview was carried out with an established jewellery company.

Business Model Canvas

To show consideration of a future business plan, part of a Business Model Canvas was completed

Diary Study

Upon receiving the item of jewellery, the case study participant was asked to complete a 'diary study' of their interactions with the piece. They were given a packet of materials – which eliminated any issues that may have arisen regarding lack of materials. A reliable participant was chosen to ensure study is carried out effectively. The qualitive data gathered here will be used to analyse the effectiveness of using natural, found materials from specific places of meaning to the user to create an item of jewellery that can be used as a tool to evoke mindfulness practices.

User Journey Map

When analysing the diary study a 'user journey map' was generated to trace specific emotions/reactions to precise moments of the case study.

Affinity Testing

To test the viability of creating a business based on creating bespoke pieces of jewellery that are made with/using natural, found materials from specific place of emotional importance to the client which can be used as a tool to evoke mindfulness, an affinity test will be carried out. Ideally a large group of participants from different educational/job sector backgrounds will be asked, covering a wider range of views. An affinity test would be simple to carry out using an indirect method. An anonymous survey was shared via social media.

Introduction

In keeping with current sustainability conversations - there has been a shift in the interest in the materials used to produce our jewellery. From the 1950s onwards the conventional roles of jewellery within society and the materials in which they are made has been challenged by so called 'artist-jewellers' (Church 2017). Many jewellers are choosing to revert to more naturally sourced materials such as wood, shells, and the like. Importantly, the consideration of the context of said materials within the piece of jewellery itself (Lagg 2008). So why not consider the significance of the place where these natural found materials are from? For centuries people have discussed their so called 'happy places'. Why not bring the memories of these places *into* jewellery for the wearer to reminisce and reflect upon during daily life? During a study on happy memories, it was revealed that 7% of participants have turned specific memories into physical mementos or stories (Wiking 2019). By having a physical connection to a place can help the user to visualise it more vividly, and visualisation goes hand-in-hand with mindfulness. The practice of mindfulness is simple yet difficult simultaneously (Kabat-Zinn 2019).

Case Study

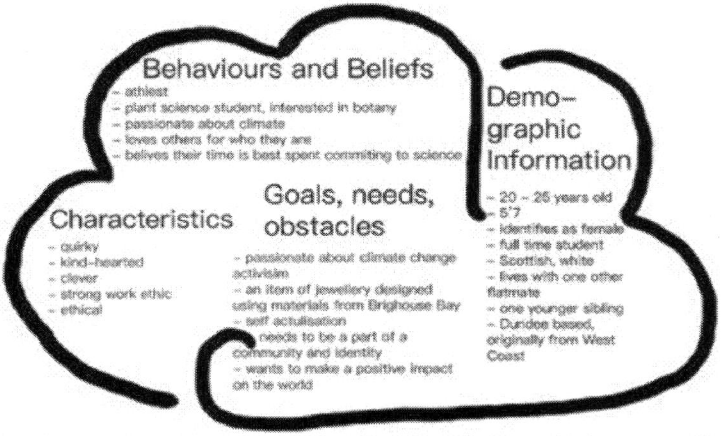

Figure 2 Persona of case study participant

The above persona shows information about the participant. It became clear that natural environments are important to them, as they are interested in botany and the impact of climate change on the environment.

The participant gave elaborate detail of their chosen place. Brighouse Bay is close to their childhood home and hosts many lovely memories of visits. Upon visiting; several stones, and a small tub of sand were collected. Allowing many different techniques of incorporating them into the design of a pinkie ring (participants chosen type of jewellery) to be considered.

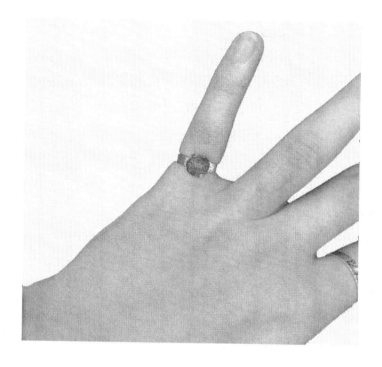

Figure 3 original ring produced for the case study

As seen in Figure 3 the pinkie ring was made in a minimalist style, yet featured bold colours of violet enamel mixed with ground down sand collected at Brighouse Bay. The participant was happy with the final design, having been asked for input in textures created in the enamelled copper dome which is set in a highly polished silver ring shank. Given that the creation of this piece was made in a mindful way with the participants exact wishes and need being considered it should inspire mindfulness practices when worn. After two days the ring was lost. As there was less time available a simpler pendent was designed and created. This time the Hand Valley pressure point was considered, Figure 4 shows the pendent in position shaped into the crevasse between the thumb and pointer finger (which is referred to as the Hand Valley pressure point). Next the copper was cleaned, a layer of transparent grey enamel fired on as a base layer, with two layers of sand fired on top. The combination of the colours of the sand contrasted nicely with the black of the oxidised copper on the edges so it was left without polishing.

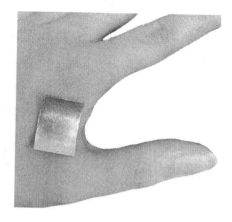

Figure 4 copper pendant placed in position on hand

Figure 5 finished sand-enamelled pendent

The participant then placed the pendent on a chain that they had been given previously by a friend – creating an additional level of emotional connection to the piece. The final stage of this case study was for the participant to wear the piece for several weeks keeping a diary study to denote the item's impact on their mindfulness practices in day-to-day life.

Amy Peoples

Use of Natural Materials in Jewellery Design

Since the earliest days of jewellery making natural resources have been used in production. Such materials as hemp, leather and ivory were used to form rings – before man discovered metals where were harder and less permeable to damage (Wang 2020). Through innovation and development production techniques have improved massively since this time. Allowing current jewellery designers to use both modern, contemporary and traditional methods in their repertoire to use natural materials with increased durability. Examples worth noting are green minerals which have been found in regular use over a variety of geography and cultures in prehistoric jewellery (Dominguez-Bella 2012). Other materials were used such as wood, shells and plant seeds; adorning people since the start of human history – used as signifiers of social hierarchies, customs and cultural values (Tsaknaki, 2015). Traditionally materials tended to be selected based on what was locally available to designers/makers as well as on their value. It is more difficult to replenish supplies of mined biproducts like silver than other more naturally reproduced resources such as shells and seeds.

Using natural, found materials within the sector of contemporary jewellery design is increasing by popular demand. As a result of the uniqueness created by using non-traditional materials in jewellery creates a large economic value (Ray, 2019). The market for jewellery comprising of alternative materials in growing. By emphasising the unique elements of the natural materials compared to the uniform of traditional cut precious stones makes it stand out. Contemporary jewellery is defined as unique design that is innovative, and understood to convey artistic expression (Ray, 2019). People wear contemporary jewellery to reflect their own artistic expression, creating an emotional connection to the piece as it reflects their personality to the outside world.

"Jewellery can be made out of almost any material, and all materials reflect the passage of time in different ways"

(Manheim, J. 2009).

By capitalising on the qualities each of these unappreciated material and processes hold, contemporary jewellery designers challenge preconceived notions of preciousness and value (Bell, 2012). Demonstrating that by featuring one-of-a-kind alternative materials unique visual qualities are created -a form of self-expression with increasing popularity.

Providing the definition of 'semi-precious gemstones' is ambiguous enough to cover a vast range of natural materials – designers can advertise many of these 'alternative' resources as 'semi-precious gemstones'. By following the logic of how gemstones are classified items such as petrified wood (which could be considered as either organic or mineral) could also be used in place of a gemstone (Vyas,

2019). Designers can increase the economic value of their work by including 'precious' when describing pieces. The value of materials can be returned by reconsidering what is defined as precious – rejuvenating these material supplies (Erl, 2011). Showing that the idea of preciousness is all about perspective. When consumers have excess money, jewellery is commonly one of the first things bought, resulting in jewellery being consumed for everyday use by more groups of people (Vyas, 2019). The days when only the rich would own valuable pieces of jewellery are past. Allowing more jewellery to be consumed by a broader range of people for everyday wear.

Connections with Jewellery

Every item of jewellery represents different potential emotional connotations. A piece of jewellery can represent a wide range of emotional connections – for example representing a specific place or metaphor, even something intangible (Romãozinho 2021). These connections are not always apparent, being very personal to the wearer. Certain gemstones evoke cultural myths and meanings. For example; sapphires are symbolic of truth, sincerity and faithfulness (Bengtsson Melin 2014). These cultural beliefs are long held having been passed down from generation to generation. Jewellery can be used to embody memories of both people we loved and the love itself (Wang 2020). Memories like these could link to any element of the jewellery; why they were given it, by whom, at what stage of their lives did they receive it and where; the aesthetics; intricate details; colour; material etc.

From an outsider's perspective these connotations are not seen, and pieces are only judged by what aesthetics are clearly visible. Allowing the wearer to keep these emotional links private – which they may share to others only if they wish to. Unlike its fashion counterparts, jewellery is less effected by popular culture and is more abiding (Romãozinho 2021). Most contemporary jewellery is designed to outlive shifting fashion movements, rebelling against the 21st century's fast fashion culture. As pieces are designed to last – opposing the planned obsolescence of modern design by utilising emotional representation and connotations.

Contradictorily – the exact opposite is asserted by fashion historians. Jewellery symbolised wealth and status instead of any sense of style, although the last century has changed this ideal and jewellery in more commonly connected to fashionable trends (Woolton 2010). In fashion-centred jewellery design there is less of an emotional focus, showing that in some jewellery design popular trends have more of an influence.

Materials used within jewellery design are impacted by the changing fashions of the time – reflecting the current opinions of society (Galton 2012). Though in situations where jewellery is mass produced to an industrial scale by large corporations this is true; smaller independent designers (e.g. Beth Lagg) are infamous for having opposing ideals - breaking away from this approach. When Fulco di Verdura started using yellow gold in his fine jewellery, his contemporaries considered him radical as during the 1940s this metal was considered common and informal (Woolton 2010). Showing there are always designers that push the boundaries of the considered norm prioritising innovative design concepts over trends.

Proving this theory; a popular movement of this decade is Extinction Rebellion, a climate change activist group, climate change awareness has increased interest in using more sustainable materials and techniques in many design sectors. Including the contemporary jewellery sector. Designers are searching for alternative approaches to have a smaller environmental and/or social impact resulting in the emergence of "eco-design", "sustainable design" etc (Moreno 2016). Current awareness and campaigns are encouraging designers to strive for more sustainable material usage. As traditional and non-renewable materials, such as silver and gold, are diminishing (Tegegne 2019). Simply put – resources are waning at a sharper rate than the current rate of consumption. Which is a direct result of planned obsolesce designs pushed out by designers. Around 40% of gold used annually comes from recycled materials (i.e. from microchips, unwanted jewellery) which has been melted down, compared to 60% newly mined gold (O'Brien 2019). Although there is an increasing interest in sustainability – contrasting activities made by fast fashion companies cannot sufficiently overcome the detrimental environmental impact created by the ever-growing industry; contemporary jewellery is trying to fight against these actions (Tegegne 2019). During the design process it is empirical that designers fully consider the entire lifecycle of all resources used. Designers should think of the ongoing life of item's materials alongside its aesthetic pleasure, convenience and usefulness (McDonough 2002). Designers would be able to instantaneously exclude specific materials by considering from the very start of their process the typical life-cycle it would have; and how it could be recycled or reused once it has reached the end of its use.

Mindfulness Practices

P racticing mindfulness helps users to relax. As to be able to properly relax you need to be aware of your own body (Kabat-Zinn, 2013). The ability to be in touch with your body is essential when using mindfulness techniques. This is the first step on anyone's mindfulness journey. Yet the idea to rapidly understand ourselves, body and mind, without experience or when in the middle of a difficult situation/surroundings can easily become overwhelming. Allowing yourself to acknowledge *every* aspect of *every* pain, comfort, itching or emotion can become all-consuming and scary. Nevertheless, this is essential for all mindfulness practices and must be aimed to achieve.

Focus is one of the main aspects of mindfulness. But this can be overwhelming. Narrowing in and focusing on objects is favoured (Verni, 2015). Being able to suddenly focus intently on oneself is a daunting task, therefore having a specific object to focus solely on is a good steppingstone to begin with. Or even for more practiced users to use when in an overwhelming situation in day-to-day life. A little nudge can be comforting and encouraging to push oneself to focus. This is the effect specific objects can have.

Another prompt that can help focus within mindfulness is visualisation. To snap your focus back into the present moment using simple visual triggers are effective reminders (Barnes, 2016). These prompts don't have to be huge, nor overly complicated. Just a simple visual stimulant that reminds the user of a specific memory or even a particular motivation. An added benefit of focusing on visualisation is creating personalised prompts unique to each user; so if one person is inspired by certain phrases/key words that can be included; whereas if someone else connects more with images/patterns they can take precedence in the design.

Benefits of using visualisation centred mindfulness are tenfold. Including reducing pain; suffering; struggles with addictions and obsessions, leading to a more productive and positive lifestyle (Gauding, 2021). Those who practice mindfulness are seeking these benefits. Combining object focused and visualisation centred mindfulness could create an entry point into the annihilating world of mindfulness. Allowing the user to ease themselves into it. Having an object that has been designed around a place in which positive memories are tied would be an approach that encapsulates the advantages of both. Giving that clear, physical connection to the place that would be visualised.

Pressure Point Research

Reflexology and acupressure are techniques used as alternative medicines. In comparison to other methods of maintaining health; hand reflexology and acupressure cause no known side effects or toxicity, nor require any specific tools (Feisong, 2019). As a result of this both methods are widely accessible and can cause no harm. The only 'tools' required generally are the users own hands (Andrews, 2007). Since no devices/tools are required, the user can carry out these treatments at their leisure or discreetly when needed. Instead of carefully inserting needles as in acupuncture, using pressure and massage actives the pressure points in acupressure (Skuban, 2018). Meaning that using acupressure can be done subtly, without drawing attention to oneself. This would benefit the user as when anxious - the idea of drawing even more attention to oneself can add to the already crushing stress levels.

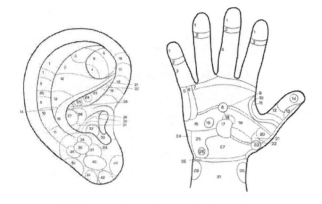

Figure 6 diagrams of reflexology points on and and ears

There are fundamental differences between how the two practices use pressure points. Both reflexology and acupressure are used to tackle health grievances and are bodywork techniques that comprise of applying pressure to precise points on the human body; although they are different as acupressure uses the entire body coming from ancient traditional medicines whereas reflexology primarily concerns using points on feet and hands with more recent

56

with roots in the last century (McMahon, No Date). Meaning that the practices tend to be used in different circumstances, depending on what is more suitable at that time.

Although both techniques reap the same benefits. Using hand reflexology and acupressure have an equivalent impact on reducing anxiety without any side effects (Vasokolaei 2017). Permitting the two methods to be interchangeable yielding the same results. These techniques are inexpensive and inclusive (Vasokolaei, 2017). Both reflexology and acupressure work with specific points on the body that directly affect different parts of the body (Teagarden, no date.). Considering social rules on what areas of the body are acceptable to touch in public this means that the user can soothe pain in any place by massaging more accessible points. These down-to-earth hands-on therapies have practical applications in daily life (Wright 2003). Which allows the user to have something to do with their hands that benefit them rather than potentially cause them harm by negative fidgeting habits such as scratching themselves.

Primary Research

Interview A

To acquire a more in-depth understanding of mindfulness, an interview took place with someone who has first-hand experiences with mindfulness techniques. Interviewee A worked in a publication about mindfulness for several years. During the interview several good points were raised. Especially explaining the true meaning of mindfulness; "Mindfulness is the inherent quality we all have to be there in the moment non-judgementally". One of the main points that became inherent during this interview was how accessible information about mindfulness is. There are multiple different types of media, such as apps, books and films. Although Interviewee A recommends not following pre-recorded sessions or practicing in an isolated setting. These less personal methods are not as successful as they do not fully consider the user's current situations, state of mind or location. This can actually have a detrimental effect on the quality of mindfulness practices, as the user may not connect as much. Another issue can be that the user is given the impression that mindfulness is about only focusing on positive thoughts and feelings. Which is not the case. Mindfulness, when practiced correctly, should be about accepting both positive and negative feelings/thoughts – being able to fully connect with oneself.

Interview B

There are misconceptions as to what is taught in undergraduate psychology, it is much more STEM based than thought. Meaning research into the effects of mindfulness is considered part of 'popular psychology', being more suited to a postgraduate study. Despite this Interviewee B explained their own experiences with mindfulness and reflexology. The practice of visualising a 'happy place' to relax was taught to Interviewee B during a maternity class rather than through their work. They consider it as more of a breathing technique – and is something they practice getting to sleep every night. Although it was agreed that some neuro-divergent people may struggle to visualise a place from scratch – and that having an item that creates a physical connection to a place would help facilitate the process. Whereas some people who have an overactive imagination would be able to use the tool to narrow their focus onto one specific place. One point that surfaced was that Interviewee B uses the movement of waves when at the beach as a breathing technique. This was an interesting point as sound can be part of visualisation, the challenge is translating sound into a still piece of jewellery. This is something that should be further explored in another study. Interviewee B has also had experience with reflexology, mainly using feet, on two separate occasions. They found the results to be astounding – as it helped sooth pain and diagnose conditions which impacted different areas of their body. When asked about whether they have a particular item of jewellery that they fiddle with to relieve stress a definite answer was given. Interestingly it was only on an occasion where they were not wearing the item they noticed their habit, which shows how unconsciously people can develop habits to combat stress ultimately creating these connections. Additionally, the idea of subtly was discussed – and how it also concerns the potential distraction of those surrounding the user. This may arise in a situation where a user is fiddling in an obvious and distracting manner that can agitate those around them. A solution to this would be that a tool created is designed to use pressure points it would be about applying pressure rather than any repetitive movements such as spinning or tapping.

Survey Findings

With the purpose of understanding what level of understanding of pressure points is common an internet survey was conducted. The findings of the survey indicated that while most people had heard of pressure points; not many could name any specific ones; nor were many fully aware of what they are used for. When given two named examples of pressure points only 18% had heard of the 'Hand Valley' point, with even less (7%) having heard of the 'Spirit Gate' point. Another finding was that the most popular type of jewellery worn are rings at 36%. Joint second were earrings and necklaces (33%). These results were interesting as it backed up some ideas; namely that most people fidget with 82.5% agreeing; also proving that pressure points are common knowledge.

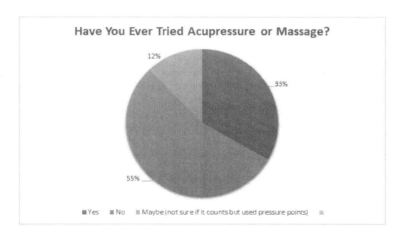

Figure 7 pie chart of survey results

However also showed that less knowledge of the use of pressure points are known with a 51:49 split. As a result of this research, introducing users to common pressure points has become another aim. To solve this, potentially, an initial idea is to include information within packaging. Such as printing a small diagram of the hand showing the most effective pressure points (Hand Valley and Spirit Gate) or having a short pamphlet.

Bespoke Business Research

Over recent years interest in bespoke designed products has been growing. Products that are individualised, customised or personalised to the buyer's needs are flourishing; with designers who adopted this approach early being able to meet or create their own demand for unique and specialised products (Cooper 2016).

Younger generations are particularly interested in standing out. To attract millennials; adopt product customisation, clear communication to create a personal connection in which they can use to help identify with the designer on a more individual level – this will help create the feel of a sustainable, luxury maker (Schemken and Berghaus 2018). By producing bespoke design based around a specific customer's needs combined with the basic design achieves a higher unique value- giving the customer extra benefits and results in a higher product value (Abdul Kudus et.al. 2016). Online selling platforms such as Esty and Not on the Highstreet have allowed customer personalisation and customisation to be more accessible to a larger number of users.

There are many benefits to having a bespoke design focused company. People are inherently different; with different needs, wants and wishes. When buying a gift for somebody who want to be unique – bespoke is the perfect choice as mass-produced work simply cannot fit this wish (McCue 2019). Treating designs with the same level of individuality as the customer allows for better customer satisfaction. This can be financially beneficial as well. When products are mass produced using expensive raw materials meaning any mistakes in the design significantly increases cost wastage. (Jepson 2020). Allowing businesses to reduce their production overheads whilst still maintaining a high quality in their finished products. When running a successful bespoke design company trust is essential; as clients must be able have trust in the designer to fulfil their specific requirements (Goulding, 2020). Considering the relationship required with the client is integral in a bespoke centred business plan, this would include contemplating the time it will take to discuss the client's needs and wishes throughout the design process to ensure the highest level of success.

The jewellery sector is budding. In contradiction to the fragility of the high street – jewellery sales have increased; as there has been an of 5% from 2018 to 2021 with two out of three UK residents purchasing jewellery or watches for gifts or themselves (Matter of Form 2021). Showing that people are still willing to spend money on adornments. In the summer of 2020 jewellery sales increased by $1,000,000,000 year over year – namely due to purchases of engagement rings (Matter of Form 2021). Consequently, it seems prudent that special fine jewellery purchases make up majority of sales. Within the jewellery sector there are many benefits to designing bespoke pieces for specific clients. Choosing bespoke designed jewellery significantly increase the level of complexity of each design and the range of materials and techniques offered (Holland 2017). More choice is suitable for a larger amount of people as it suits more needs than simply providing a small, concise range. When working metal by hand makes it stronger as it is hardened more effectively and is less porous – meaning it is more inherently durable than machine-made mass-produced work (Gearing 2018). Durability is a common consideration when purchasing jewellery as the buyer would consider this better value for money.

Comparatively, bespoke companies in the fashion industry are also gaining interest.

Recently because of diminishing interest in casual clothing, there has been a developing recognition and appreciation for the tradition of bespoke tailoring (Almond 2011). Turning the direction of trends to fight against the onslaught of fast fashion and it's devastating environmental impacts. Choosing to buy tailored clothes rather than mass-produced clothing is a conscious choice as each item is fitted to the buyer's precise body measurements – reducing waste (Dressarte, no date). Granting small changes in people's attitudes and habits whilst giving a sense of satisfaction that they are benefitting from a conscious choice to help the environment. Electing to buy bespoke garments allows the buyer to select the highest-quality materials, fit for purpose for precious life moments (Stone 2021). Again, adding another valuable element to entice customers to dismiss mass-produced items for bespoke work.

Example Spinner Ring

American jewellery brand Jane Loren focuses solely on creating a collection of rings advertised as 'anti-anxiety fidgets' (2022). They also promote the fact that they are a female owned company, aiming to enhance body positivity and calmness. All their rings are made using titanium steel (which is commonly referred to as hypoallergenic); most rings are adjustable; with the fixed sized rings available in six sizes.

Figure 8 Jane Loren 'Loren Adjustable Spinner Ring in Stardust'

Figure 8 shows one such product from their site. This particular ring comes in three different details (Stardust, Free Bird and Phases). It is a spinner ring, meaning it is made in two separate ring shanks that are connected in such a way that they can move independently of each other. Spinner rings are commonly known as 'fidget rings', although this one is actively described as 'anti-anxiety'.

Figure 9 Spinner Ring from different brand

Comparatively, this spinner ring is more traditional in style and is branded as such. Although it still describes itself as a "worry ring", tracing back to its routes in traditional meditation used in ancient Tibet (Orli, 2022). This company fits more into the category of fine jewellery as it uses precious metals (silver and gold plating) compared to titanium.

Example Bespoke Jewellery Company

There are several jewellery companies in the UK that work solely on bespoke commissions. One such company is Harriet Kelsall Bespoke Jewellery which was founded in 1998. Since then, they have received plenty of recognition – including winning Bespoke Jeweller of the Year during the pandemic in 2020. They have also been awarded a Responsible Jewellery Council Certification, making them the first jewellery company worldwide to be both Fairtrade certified and responsible. The success of this company proves that a business can survive and thrive providing only bespoke work.

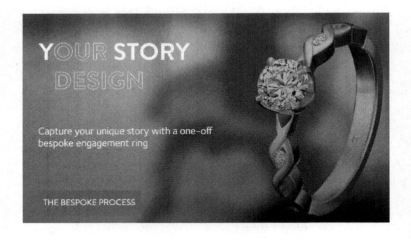

Figure 10 screenshot from Harriet Kelsall Bespoke Jewellery website

After approaching the company with some questions over email the Head of Design and Production graciously answered. Giving a fantastic inside-view of the way the company runs and approaches the processing of designing bespoke work.

They explained that whilst birthday and anniversary gifts alongside memorial jewellery have increased in popularity in recent years; the most popular pieces commissioned are engagement rings, wedding rings and eternity rings.

The rise in social media platforms, namely Pinterest and Instagram, has allowed customers to work exactly what styles attract them. There has also been a growing societal trend in people adopting more individualistic styles and designs rather than following trends of established brands and design for themselves rather than following brands. This has led to a significant growth within Harriet Kelsall and other companies offering bespoke services.

The Head of Design and Production has credited the success of the company to their considerable experience designing bespoke commissions— amassing over 25,000 commissions throughout its history. Describing their style as 'clean sheet bespoke jewellers' - meaning the process is quite literally started with a blank sheet of paper instead of a checklist of pre-determined designs - the price of each commission is calculated separately based on hours of work, general workshop/business overheads, materials and production costs. Initially they take a deposit for any starting sketches created by their team of twenty designers; although this is taken off the final price of the piece if customers proceed with the design to account for the time taken to design. As a part of their Responsible Jewellery pledge, they also offer to re-use stones and precious metals from customer's old jewellery, which is a service some other jewellery companies choose to avoid.

Proposed Solution

Introduction to People in the Clouds

Whilst the proposed business will produce jewellery – as it each piece will be specifically designed for individual users it is best to take a more product (UX) design approach when formulating a business proposal. The name for said company is 'People in the Clouds', which was created using word play on the saying 'head in the clouds' to describe someone who is distracted. Figure 11 below shows a sketch of a potential logo.

Figure 11 draft logo for proposed company People in the Clouds

As this company will operate as a small business (with only one main designer initially) the simple, sketch like style of the logo has been used to seem more personal to gain an preliminary following on social medias such as Instagram and Facebook. Business cards have been distributed in small, independently-owned shops in the South Side of Glasgow – namely Shawlands to test interest of shoppers who would be interested in local designers.

Business Model Canvas

One common method of displaying a proposed business idea is through drawing a Business Model Canvas (BMC). This covers the key areas that must be considered when creating a start-up, highlighting areas that need further attention and solutions to any potential issues.

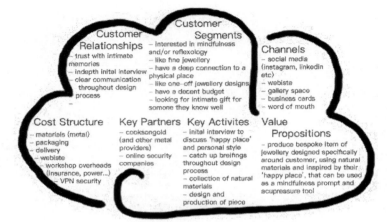

Figure 12 proposed BMC for People in the Clouds

A potential issue would be the actual collection of the natural material samples. Say the client's special place is somewhere that is difficult to access or too far away to travel to; then a proposed solution would be to send packaging to the client for them to post the materials in. If this situation arises then it would be considered in the final cost of the product as an overhead.

When sending the final product to the client a personalised pamphlet of how their specific piece can be used regarding pressure points will come within the packaging. As well as a brief introduction to visualisation-based mindfulness. This information would enhance their mindfulness experience, as it became apparent through research that this is a more engaging approach.

The channels essential to the running of this business would be finding a reliable delivery company that offers secure delivery. Another key channel would be online security, to protect the users' virtual private network (VPN), bank details and meet general data protection regulations (GDPR) standards. This would also protect any virtual calls – for example if the initial interview about their happy place was to be carried out online rather than in-person. Interviews done this way would reduce the need for an office space, meaning only a workshop would need to be rented and/or insured. A website with a clear, easy to navigate interface would also be essential.

As this work would be bespoke, products would be displayed in galleries as photographs. Meaning that it would have to be weighed against having a mainly online presence. This would depend on the footfall of each gallery in question.

Testing Solution

Diary Study

From the 11th of November until the 20th of December the participant completed a diary study. This revealed personal insights into the effect of using on mindfulness. On the first day alone, the participant stated that they felt like;

'I have a piece of home with me'

Connection to place is vital to this project, and this sentence proves that this has been successful.

The pendent was meant to be reminiscent of the surroundings where the sand was collected from. This aspect of the design came through successfully as it;

'Makes me feel like I picked something up from off the beach'

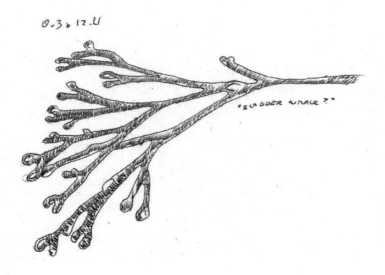

Figure 13, Drawing from Diary Study by Participant

Regarding the impact of the pendent to their mental health they described it as;

> **'Always such a relief to bring my hand**
> **to my chest and find this pendant'**

Which is a great success as this is exactly what the intention of this whole project was. To positively improve the wearer's metal health by harnessing the power of happy memories, and their connection to a specific place.

User Journey Map

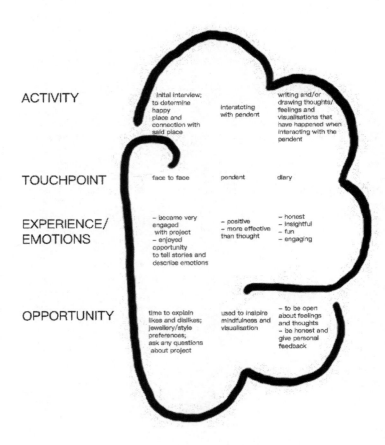

Figure 14 User Journey map of participant

This User Journey Map follows the participant's journey throughout the different stages of the case study. Interestingly, it was only once the participant started interacting with the pendent that they fully grasped the potential of using natural materials from their happy place. As a result, the whole project was realised to be more effective than initially thought.

Affinity Testing

Using an anonymous online survey data was collected asking participants to answer using their initial instincts to questions.

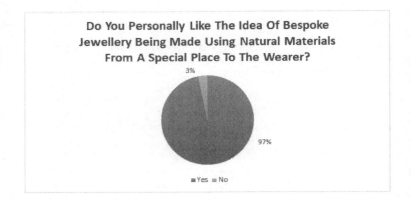

Figure 15 pie chart of survey results

Only two out of sixty-two people asked didn't like the idea of creating a item of bespoke jewellery using natural materials from a special place to the wearer. This may be a result of some participants being more sentimental than others, or a lack of interest in bespoke jewellery.

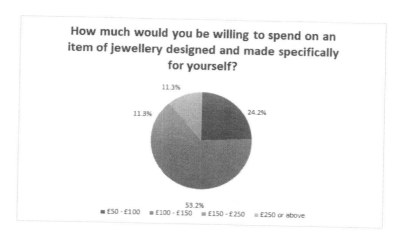

Figure 16 pie chart of survey results

Whereas there was a less clear answer regarding how much people were willing to spend. Whilst the category of £100-£150 was significantly higher than the others (at 53.2%), two other categories were evenly split at 11.3% (£150-£250 and £250 or above respectively) of 62 people asked. The lowest price range of £50-£100 took 24.2% of the votes.

Conclusion

I n conclusion, by incorporating natural, found materials from specific locations of emotional value into bespoke jewellery- creates an effective tool to evoke mindfulness practices to improve mental health in daily life. Which could also lead to a viable business venture. To test the potential procedures this business would take, a case study was conducted. Whilst using natural materials in jewellery is not a new concept, having been done for centuries, applying it as an emotional catalyst in contemporary fine jewellery would supplement an additional level of value to a piece – both economically and emotionally. Mindfulness, acupressure, and reflexology are non-medical interventions to improve general health. They are non-evasive techniques that do not require any tools nor training. Interviews were performed between two people with entirely different backgrounds on mindfulness.

Although interestingly they both yielded strikingly similar opinions – that mindfulness effects individual people differently but has inherently positive results. It became apparent that there is a general lack of understanding and knowledge regarding acupressure points, with survey results showing around half of participants were not sure what their uses and benefits are. Bespoke work is increasing in popularity over a wide range of businesses. This is due to its effects on reducing overheads and production costs, as well as customers looking for higher quality items that are sustainable and unique. Jewellery touted as anti-anxiety exists already but depends on the marketing and advertising to convince the user as such. The sector of bespoke jewellery design is a booming market. The success of companies such as Harriet Kelsall demonstrates this, also showing the longevity of such success since launching in 1998.

People in the Clouds has been created to fills this potential gap in the market.

Ideally - a larger number of case studies would have been carried out. Including a variety of age, gender, preferences, neurotypical compared to neuro-divergent, budget, and actual type of natural materials themselves. In future, creating some prototypes for the user to try would be an informative extra step in the process. Another aspect that should be farther considered in future studies is adding elements of auditory stimulation. Findings have shown that such an item of jewellery can create a stronger connection to place. The case study participant found that the pendent had a large impact on mindfulness to them, also prompting intense emotional reactions when interacting with the pendent. The pendent was successful in stimulating strong visualisations of their happy place – even just by remembering that they were wearing it evoked visual, olfactory, auditory, and sensory memories. By using an affinity test it has also been proven that there is a general interest in this idea.

Reference List

Abdul Kudus, S. I., Campbell, R. I. and Bibb, R. (2016) *Customer Perceived Value for Self-designed Personalised Products Made Using Additive Manufacturing.* International Journal of Industrial Engineering and Management (IJIEM), Vol. 7 No 4, 2016, pp. 183-193 Available at: www.iim.ftn.uns.ac.rs/ijiem_journal.php [Last Accessed 28th April 2021] ISSN 2217-2661

Almond, K. (2011) *Bespoke Tailoring: the luxury and heritage we can afford* Available at; https://eprints.hud.ac.uk/id/eprint/13855/1/Microsof t_Word_-_Hand_Crafted_Tailoring_versus_phd_1.pdf (Last Accessed on 11th November 2021)

Andrews, S. and Dempsey B. (2007) *Acupressure & Reflexology for Dummies.* New Jersey, United States: Wiley Publishing Inc.

Barnes, A. (2016) *How to Be Mindful.* London, United Kingdom: Vie Books, an imprint of Summersdale Publishers. Page 17

Bell, R. A. (2012).*Fragmentation and the found in the production of contemporary jewellery.* (Unpublished document submitted in partial fulfilment of the requirements for the degree of Master of Design). Unitec Institute of Technology, Auckland, New Zealand. Available at: https://hdl.handle.net/10652/1914 [Last Accessed 27th April 2021]

Bengtsson Melin, P. (2014) *For love, healing and protection. Notes on Medieval finger rings with sapphires and other gemstones in Swedish collections.* Available at: http://samla.raa.se/xmlui/bitstream/handle/raa/8409/2014_259.pdf [Last Accessed 22nd April 2021]

Cooper, F. (2016) *Sintering and additive manufacturing: "additive manufacturing and the new paradigm for the jewellery manufacturer".* Available at: https://link.springer.com/content/pdf/10.1007/s40964-015-0003-2.pdf [Last Accessed 28th April 2021]

Dominguez-Bella, S. (2012) *Archaeomineralogy of prehistoric artifacts and gemstones.* Available at: http://www.ehu.eus/sem/seminario_pdf/SeminSEMv9p5-28.pdf [Last Accessed 27th April 2021]

Dressarte (no date) Available at: https://www.dressarteparis.com/benefits-of-bespoke-clothes/ [Last Accessed 23rd November 2021]

Erl, I.M. (2011) *Street Combing: An investigation into the use of found materials from the urban landscape in contemporary jewellery making.* (Unpublished document submitted in partial fulfilment of the requirements for the degree of Master of Design). Unitec Institute of Technology. Available at: https://hdl.handle.net/10652/1922 [Last Accessed 29th April 2021]

Feisong, C. and Guozhong, G. (2019) *Hand Reflexology & Acupressure: A Natural Way to Health Through Traditional Chinese Medicine.* New York, United States of America: Better Link Press. Pg 7

Galton, E. (2012) *Basics Fashion Design 10: Jewellery Design: From Fashion to Fine Jewellery.* Bloomsbury. Basics Fashion Design Vol. 10

Gauding, M. (2021) *The Meditation Experience.* London, United Kingdom: Octopus Publishing Group Limited. Revised Edition page 156

Gearing, J. (2018) *Handmade vs Cast Jewellery* Available at: https://www.jodiegearing.com/handmade-vs-cast-jewellery/ (Last Accessed 23rd November 2021)

Goulding, S. (2020) *Manufacturing & Production: Engineering Magazine* Available at; https://mpemagazine.co.uk/2020/07/29/bespoke-manufacturing/ (Last Accessed 9th November 2021)

Holland, C. (2017*) Cast vs Handmade: How we make our jewellery pieces* Available at; https://www.carolyncodd.com/blogs/news/cast-vs-handmade-how-we-make-our-jewellery-pieces (Last Accessed 10th November 2021)

Jepson, P. (2020) *EGL Vaughan* Available at; https://eglvaughan.co.uk/bespoke-engineering-7-advantages/ (Last Accessed 9th November 2021)

Kabat-Zinn, J. (2013) *Full Catastrophe Living: Using the Wisdom of Your Body and Mind to Face Stress, Pain, and Illness.* New York, United States of America: Bantam Books. Revised Edition

Kabat-Zinn, J. (2019) *Wherever You Go, There You Are.* London, United Kingdom: Piatkus. Revised Edition

Manheim, J. (2009) *Sustainable Jewellery*. London. A&C Black Publishers Ltd.

Matter of Form (2021) *The Future of the Jewellery Industry: Trends & Insights* Available at; https://www.matterofform.com/news/articles/jewellery-industry-trends (Last Accessed 10th November 2021)

McCue, L. (2019) *Fine Bespoke Jewellery – The Benefits* Available at; https://houseofmccue.co.uk/benefits-of-bespoke-jewellery/ (Last Accessed 10th November 2021)

McDonough, W. and Braungart ,M. (2002) *Cradle to Cradle*. United States of America: North Point Press. Page 63

McMahon, M. (No Date) *What Is the Difference between Reflexology and Acupressure?* Available at: https://www.thehealthboard.com/what-is-the-difference-between-reflexology-and-acupressure.htm [Last Accessed 23rd November 2021]

Moreno, M., De los Rios, C., Rowe, Z. and Charnley, F.A. (2016) 'Chapter 8: Sustainability' *Conceptual Framework for Circular Design*. Available at: https://doi.org/10.3390/su8090937 [Last Accessed April 22nd 2021]

O'Brien, K. (2019) *Top 10 Facts About Fairtrade* Gold Available at: https://www.fairtrade.org.uk/media-centre/blog/top-10-facts-about-fairtrade-gold/ [Last Accessible 23rd November 2021]

Orli Jewellery (2022) *Sterling Silver Spinner Ring With Gold Bands* Available at; https://www.orlijewellery.com/products/sterling-silver-spinner-ring-with-yellow-gold-bands?variant=39515711471719&utm_campaign=gs-2018-09-21&utm_source=google&utm_medium=smart_campaign&gclid=CjwKCAiA0KmPBhBqEiwAJqKK47CU_BsZ_fnMXFb5m-H1U8oM37l8azkYC2fbgPDiVTTknh_7DlHmbxoC3KcQAvD_BwE [Last accessed : 21st January 2022]

Rahmani Vasokolaei, Z., Rejeh, N., Heravi-Karimooi, M., Tadrisi, S.D., Kiarash Saatchi,[4] Zahra Poshtchaman,[5] Christina Sieloff,[6] and Mojtaba Vaismoradi (2017) *Comparison of the Effects of Hand Reflexology versus Acupressure on Anxiety and Vital Signs in Female Patients with Coronary Artery Diseases.* US National Library of Medicine National Institutes of Health. Available at: https://www.ncbi.nlm.nih.gov/pmc/articles/PMC6473738/ (Last Accessed 11th November 2021)

Ray, S. (2019) *New trend in Jewelry industry and Sustainable materials to develop lifestyle products.* Available at: https://www.researchgate.net/publication/332672275_New_trend_in_Jewelry_industry_and_Sustainable_materials_to_develop_lifestyle_products [Last Accessed Feb 26 2021].

Romãozinho M. (2021) *Sustainability in Jewellery Design Process: Reusing and Reinventing.* In: Raposo D., Neves J., Silva J., Correia Castilho L., Dias R. (eds) Advances in Design, Music and Arts. EIMAD 2020. Springer Series in Design and Innovation, vol 9. Springer, Cham.

Available at: https://doi.org/10.1007/978-3-030-55700-3_28 [Last Accessed 9th April 2021]

Schemken, M. and Berghaus, B. (2018) *The Relevance of Sustainability in Luxury from the Millennials' Point of View.* In: Gardetti M., Muthu S. (eds) Sustainable Luxury, Entrepreneurship, and Innovation. Environmental Footprints and Eco-design of Products and Processes. Springer, Singapore. Available at: https://doi.org/10.1007/978-981-10-6716-7_6 [Last Accessed 28th April 2021]

Skuban, R. (2018) *What are the Benefits of Acupressure?* Miami Massage College Available at: https://www.amcollege.edu/blog/benefits-of-acupressure [Last Accessed 23rd November 2021]

Stone, S. (2021) *The Benefits of Bespoke Clothing to Take Note of* Available at; https://www.fibre2fashion.com/industry-article/8997/the-benefits-of-bespoke-clothing-to-take-note-of [Last Accessed 23rd Novemeber 2021]

Teagarden, K (N/A) *How Does Reflexology Work?* Available at: https://www.takingcharge.csh.umn.edu/explore-healing-practices/reflexology/how-does-reflexology-work [Last Accessed 11th November 2021]

Tegegne, S. (2019) *Sustainable Jewellery – An Alternative Approach to Sustainability in Jewellery.* Politecnico Milano. Available at: http://hdl.handle.net/10589/151991 [Last Accessed 28th April 2021]

Tsaknaki, V., Frenaeus, Y. and Jonsson, M. (2015) *Precious Materials of Interaction: Exploring Interactive Accessories as Jewellery Items.* Available at:

https://www.researchgate.net/publication/285397028_Precious_Materials_of_Interaction_Exploring_Interactive_Accessories_as_Jewellery_Items No 6 (2015): Nordes 2015: Design Ecologies, ISSN 1604-9705. Stockholm [Last Accessed 28th April 2021]

Vasokolaei, Z. R., Rejeh, N., Heravi-Karimooi, M., Tadrisi, S. D., Saatchi, K., Poshtchaman, Z., Sieloff, C. and Vaismorandi, M. (2017) *Comparison of the Effects of Hand Reflexology versus Acupressure on Anxiety and Vital Signs in Female Patients with Coronary Artery Diseases.* US National Library of Medicine National Institutes of Health. Available at: https://www.ncbi.nlm.nih.gov/pmc/articles/PMC6473738/ [Last Accessed 23rd November 2021]

Verni, K. A. (2015) *Practical Mindfulness: A Step-by-Step Guide.* London, United Kingdom: Dorling Kindersley Limited. Page 11

Vyas P.K. (2019) *Proposition of a Selection Matrix for Use of Nonconventional Materials in Jewellery and Ornamental Applications.* Available at: https://link.springer.com/chapter/10.1007/978-981-13-5974-3_43 [Last Accessed April 5th 2021]

Wang, Y. (2020) *Sentimental expression in jewelry design.* Available at: https://www.politesi.polimi.it/handle/10589/153690?mode=complete [Last Accessed April 22nd 2021]

Woolton, C (2010) *Fashion for Jewels.* London: Prestel Publishing Ltd.

Wright, J. (2003) *Reflexology and Acupressure* London, United Kingdom: Octopus Publishing Group

Acknowledgements

I would like to thank; my dissertation supervisor Dr Frances Stevenson for helping me structure, plan and finalise my ideas into a successful project proposal; my wonderful case study participant Hazel Sturgess; and those who took the time to answer my surveys and interviews (namely Dr Anne Scrimgeour, Claire Littlefair and Rebecca Howarth).

Examples of Author's Work

Amy Peoples

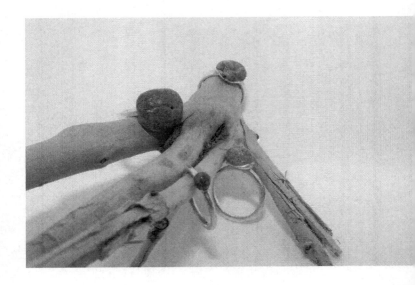

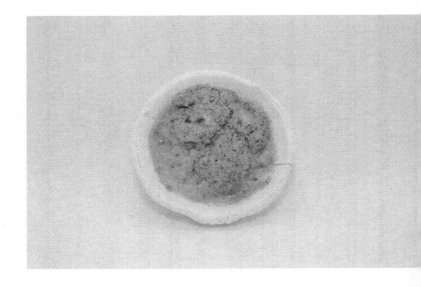

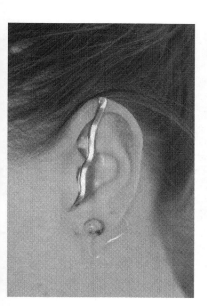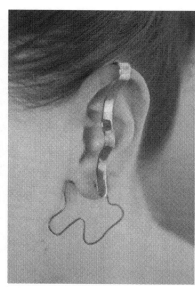

Amy Peoples

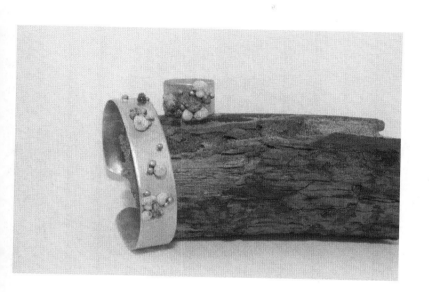

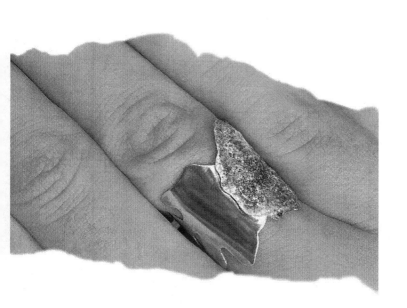

BOOM!

This book was originally submitted as a dissertation in partial fulfilment of the requirements of a Bachelor of Arts (Hons) degree in Jewellery and Metal Design at the Duncan of Jordanstone College of Art and Design, the University of Dundee, in 2022.

A note about Boom Graduates

We propel graduates forward so they can make their mark on the world - we push the boundaries, share brilliant ideas and inspire possibility. We publish dissertations as books, presented gift-boxed at graduation ceremonies, delivering brand-new research to the world quicker than anyone else. We plant trees for every commissioned book sold, and give our Boom graduates the chance to profit-share from their brilliant ideas. Furthermore we donate the majority of our profits to funding research and scholarship for disadvantaged students who wouldn't normally be able to attend university. Through academic excellence and environmental sustainability, *Boom Graduates* are changing the world.

We are Boom Graduates - an imprint of Boom Publications Ltd. We are a more-than-profit company, dedicating over half our profits to providing university scholarships for underprivileged students across the world. We aim to become the globe's biggest provider of such scholarships – and if like Amy, the author of this book, you'd also like to contribute to making the world a better place, please contact us: we publish monographs, edited books, and moreover our graduate series – Boom Graduates – are presented at graduation days across the world in archival, lined museum-quality presentation cases, engraved with the graduate's name and award.

Boom Publications are based at the Duncan of Jordanstone College of Art and Design, at the University of Dundee in Scotland. We were one of the winners of the 2022 Venture awards hosted by the Centre for Entrepreneurship, and have since been shortlisted for the Converge Challenge, a national award that brings together ambitious and creative thinkers with innovative ideas to work with industry experts to transform their ideas into sustainable companies operating in the commercial world. We are also climate conscious and work with agencies to plant a tree for each and every book commissioned, offsetting thousands of tonnes of carbon each year. Follow us on social media to watch our forest grow @boomgraduates.

Thank you for contributing by purchasing this book. Please visit our catalogues on www.boompublications.com.

Notes

Amy Peoples

Amy Peoples

Amy Peoples

Printed in Great Britain
by Amazon

16329196R00079